JASON JESSUP

Everyday Trivia: Bringing the Brain Back to Life

365 Trivia Questions And Fun Facts For All Ages, All Year Long

This book was professionally typeset on Reedsy.
Find out more at reedsy.com

Contents

1

Introduction: Let the Trivia Begin!

Welcome to your new daily brain booster! **"Everyday Trivia: Bringing the Brain Back to Life"** isn't just a trivia book; it's a fun-filled journey through the world's most fascinating facts and stories. Why did I write this book? To spark curiosity, to entertain, and to share the importance of discovering something new every day!

In this book, you'll find <u>365</u> trivia questions and facts, covering everything from the quirks of everyday life to the wonders of science and technology, the excitement of sports, the beauty of nature, and the allure of arts and literature. There's something here for everyone, no matter your age or interests.

Each chapter is crafted to not just offer you facts but to tell a story, to connect the dots in a way that makes learning fun and effortless. You'll find yourself armed with conversation starters, party tricks, and perhaps a deeper appreciation for the world we live in.

Think of this book as your daily mental gymnastics routine, designed to educate, entertain, and maybe even make you smile a bit. Whether you're a trivia newbie or a seasoned pro, you're in for a treat. So, let's turn the page and start our journey with **"Everyday Life"**. Get ready to learn, laugh, and see the world from a whole new perspective. I encourage you to follow along and guess the questions before revealing the answers. Trivia time starts now!

2

Everyday Life Curiosities

Welcome to the chapter that celebrates the extraordinary in the ordinary – Everyday Life. Here, we dive into the curious aspects of our daily routines, uncovering fun facts and nifty hacks that make regular life anything but mundane. Get ready to test your knowledge and maybe even pick up a few life-changing tricks along the way!

Everyday Life Trivia Questions:

1. What common household item can you use to remove permanent marker stains?

2. How many times does the average person laugh in a day?

3. What is the most popular day of the week for grocery shopping?

4. In what country was the toothbrush invented?

5. What percentage of our waking hours are spent in front of digital screens?

6. Which common kitchen ingredient can be used to clean silverware?

7. How long does it take for a plastic bottle to decompose?

8. What is the most frequently lost household item?

9. What color are aircraft black boxes actually?

10. What is the best angle to use when sharpening kitchen knives?

11. How many times heavier is the average adult brain compared to a newborn's?

12. What fruit can be used to tenderize meat?

13. Which side of aluminum foil is more effective in retaining heat?

14. What day of the week are most heart attacks reported to happen?

15. How many times does the average person touch their face each day?

16. Which household chore burns the most calories?

17. What's the best way to increase the lifespan of razor blades?

18. What can you use apple cider vinegar for in laundry?

19. What is the most left-behind item in hotels?

20. How long does the average person spend waiting at red lights in their lifetime?

21. On average, how many times in a day do Americans open up the fridge?

22. What is the most common time for wake-up alarms to be set worldwide?

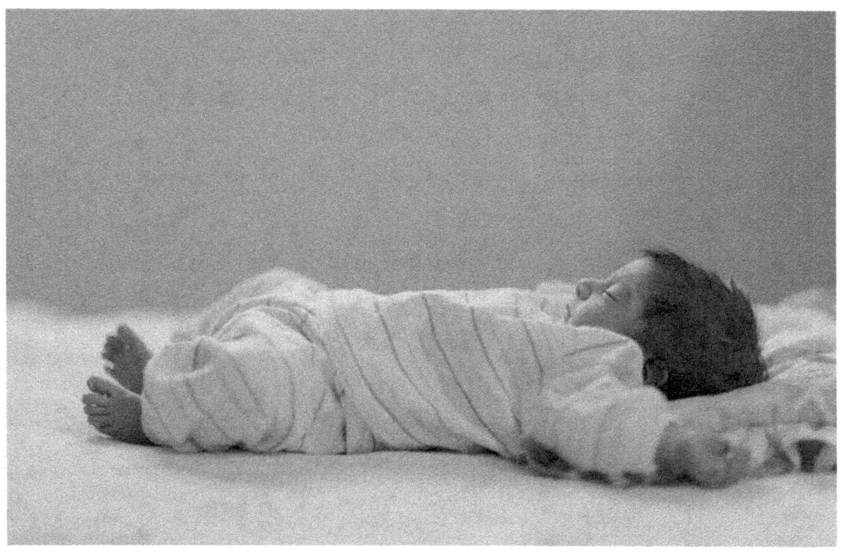

Everyday Life Answers:

1. **Toothpaste** – it's surprisingly effective on most surfaces!
2. The average person laughs **13** times a day.
3. **Saturday** is the busiest day for grocery-shopping.
4. The toothbrush was invented in **China.**
5. Approximately **60%** of our waking hours.
6. **Baking soda** – just make a paste with water and gently rub.
7. It takes **up to 450 years** for a plastic bottle to decompose.
8. **Keys** are the most frequently lost household item.
9. Aircraft black boxes are actually **bright orange** for visibility.
10. A **20-degree angle** is ideal for sharpening kitchen knives.
11. The adult brain is about **three times** heavier than a newborn's.
12. **Pineapple** – it contains an enzyme called bromelain that breaks down protein.
13. The **shiny side** of aluminum foil retains heat better.

14. Most heart attacks occur on **Monday**.

15. On average, people touch their face **23 times per hour**.

16. **Vacuuming** burns the most calories among common household chores.

17. Storing razor blades in a **dry environment** helps increase their lifespan.

18. Apple cider vinegar can be used as a natural **fabric softener** in laundry.

19. **Phone chargers** are the most left-behind item in hotels.

20. The average person spends **about 6 months** of their life waiting at red lights.

21. In America, the fridge gets opened about **22 times** in a day.

22. The most common alarm time is set for **7:00 AM.**

Armed with these everyday trivia gems and hacks, you're set to be the star of any casual conversation. Stay tuned for the next chapter, where we dive into the fascinating world of **Science and Technology**. Let's keep the trivia train moving!

3

Wonders of Science and Technology

Strap in for a curious ride through the realms of Science and Technology! In this chapter, we're not just exploring the wonders of tech and science; we're delving into its odd corners, unearthing trivia questions that will make you think, chuckle, and maybe even go, "Huh?!"

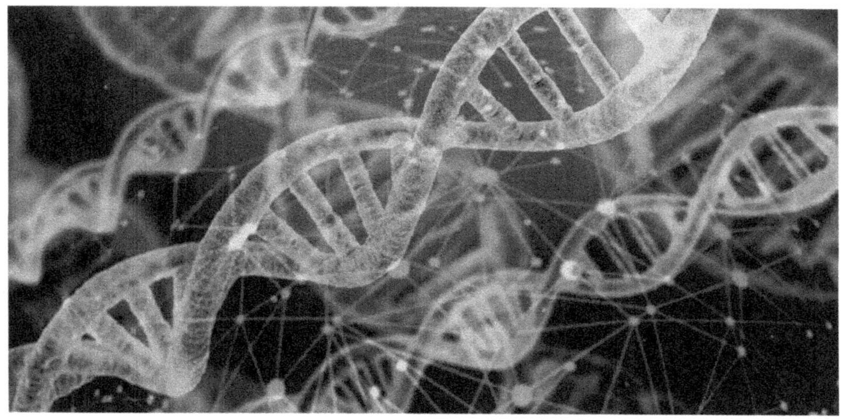

Scientific Trivia Questions:

1. What does Wi-Fi actually stand for?
2. What was the first message ever sent via text?
3. How much does a standard NASA space suit cost?
4. What is the speed of light in miles per second?
5. When was the first email sent, and what did it say?
6. How much was the first piece of art created by artificial intelligence sold for?
7. Who is often referred to as the father of the internet?
8. What year was the first mobile phone invented?
9. What was the first video game ever made?
10. What was the original name of the search engine Google?
11. In which year was the first robot created?
12. What was the first image ever uploaded to the internet?
13. When was the first Bitcoin ever mined?
14. When was the first Bitcoin purchase? And what was purchased?
15. How much voltage can an electric eel generate?
16. How long does it take for light to travel from the moon to Earth?
17. What was the first food intentionally cooked in a microwave?
18. What was the first emoji ever created?
19. What was the first actual computer "bug"?
20. What was the weight of the first ever computer used to connect to the internet?
21. What percentage of people admit to being addicted to their digital devices?
22. When was the first brain surgery performed?
23. How long did the longest-lasting light bulb last?
24. What was the first song played on the moon?
25. What was the first computer password ever used?

Answers with a Science Twist:

1. Wi-Fi stands for **Wireless Fidelity**. Who knew?
2. The first text message was **"Merry Christmas."** Simple, yet historic.
3. A NASA space suit costs about **$12 million**. Talk about out-of-this-world pricing!
4. **186,282 miles per second**. Yes, light is the ultimate speedster.
5. In **1971**, the message was **"QWERTYUIOP."** Not exactly Shake-

speare.

6. **$432,500**. That AI might just quit its day job.

7. **Vint Cerf** is the co-designer of the TCP/IP protocols and the architecture of the Internet. Thanks, Vint!

8. On April 3, **1973**, Martin Cooper stood on a sidewalk on sixth avenue in Manhattan with a device the size of a brick and made the first public call.

9. The first video game created was **1958's Tennis for Two**, featuring moving graphics on an oscilloscope, like an earlier version of "Pong".

10. It was called **"Backrub."** Not creepy at all.

11. In **1921**. And no, it didn't do the dishes.

12. An **image** of a **comedy band** called Les Horribles Cernettes **in 1992**. Rock on!

13. Satoshi Nakamoto mined the Genesis Block on **Jan. 3, 2009**. And now it's the digital gold rush.

14. On **May 22, 2010** Laszlo Hanyecz paid Jeremy Sturdivant **10,000** bitcoins (BTC) for **two** Papa John's **pizzas** which were delivered to Hanyecz's home.

15. **Up to 600 volts**. Shocking, isn't it?

16. **About 1.3 seconds.** Faster than microwaving popcorn.

17. **Popcorn**. And thus, movie night was revolutionized.

18. **A smiley face**. (:

19. **A real moth** was found in a computer in 1947. Debugging, literally.

20. **Over 2 tons**. That's one heavy email!

21. **About 66%**. The other 34% couldn't answer because they were checking their phones.

22. **Around 7,000 years ago**. Ancient brainiacs at work.

23. Over **110** years and still glowing. Talk about energy efficiency!

24. **"Fly Me to the Moon."** Classic.

25. **"Password."** Creativity wasn't high on the agenda.

And there you have it – a heap of high-tech trivia to impress your friends and maybe even win a pub quiz or two. Next chapter, we're jumping into the realm of Sports and Games, where athleticism meets amusement. Game on!

4

Sports and Games- Playful Competition

Welcome to the playful arena of Sports and Games, where athleticism meets amusement in the most unexpected ways. In this chapter, we dive into trivia questions that will test your knowledge of sports and games, sprinkled with a healthy dose of humor and surprise.

Sports Trivia Questions:

1. What was the first Olympic sport to allow women to compete?
2. How many dimples does a standard golf ball have?
3. Why were the first marathons 26.2 miles long?
4. Which two countries used ping pong to improve their relations in the 1970s?
5. What geometric shape is found on a traditional soccer ball?
6. What was the first ball used in basketball?
7. Who holds the record for the fastest serve in tennis?
8. What sport was played on the moon by an astronaut?
9. Which NFL Franchise has won the most Super Bowl trophies?
10. How long did the longest tennis match last?
11. Who is the oldest person to ever win an Olympic medal?
12. What was the duration of the longest cricket match ever played?
13. What was the first video game to be played in space?
14. Why is a rugby ball oval-shaped?
15. At what temperature are hockey pucks frozen before a game?
16. In what sport is it illegal to play left-handed?
17. Why was volleyball originally invented?
18. What were billiard balls originally made from?
19. Who was the first woman to win an Olympic gold medal?
20. Which sport is known for having the most rules?
21. How did athletes compete in the ancient Olympics?
22. Where is the world's deepest swimming pool located?
23. What was the first sport to be featured on a postage stamp?
24. What is the rarest play in baseball?

Sports and Games Answers:

1. **Tennis**, in the 1900 Olympics.
2. On average, a standard golf ball has **336 dimples**.
3. To **match** the **distance** from **Marathon to Athens**.
4. The **United States and China** used ping pong to improve their relations in 1971.
5. **Pentagons** are found on a traditional soccer ball.
6. A **soccer ball** was the first ball used in basketball.
7. The fastest serve in tennis is from **Sam Groth**, at **163.7 mph**.
8. **Golf** was the first sport played on the moon, by Alan Shepard.
9. The **New England Patriots** have won the Super Bowl a record **six times**, all with NFL Legend, Tom Brady.
10. The longest tennis match ever was **11 hours and 5 minutes.**
11. **Oscar Swahn** was 72 years old when he won a silver medal in an Olympic shooting event.
12. The longest cricket match ever lasted **10 days**! Crazy!

13. The first video game played in space was **Tetris**, on the **Mir space station**.
14. The oval shape is useful for players as the ball is **easier to handle and hold** it whilst running.
15. Frozen to **14 degrees Fahrenheit**.
16. The rules of **Polo** specify that the mallet must be held only in the right-hand for safety reasons.
17. So that people who found **basketball's** 'bumping' or 'jolting' too strenuous could have an **alternative** physical activity to fall back on.
18. **Elephant ivory** was favored for billiard balls from at least 1627 until the early 20th century.
19. **Hélène de Pourtalès** was the first woman to compete at the Olympics and the first female Olympic gold medalist.
20. **Cricket** is known for having the most rules.
21. **Naked**! Quite the spectacle!
22. In **Dubai, United Arab Emirates,** the pool goes down to about 197 feet and contains roughly 3.7 million gallons of water.
23. **Baseball** was the first sport to be featured on a postage stamp.
24. A **triple play** without an assist or putout.

And there you have it – a collection of sports and games trivia that's as entertaining as it is enlightening. Up next, we're venturing into the wild world of Animals and Nature. Stay tuned for more fun facts and quirky questions!

5

Animals and Nature - In The Wild

Prepare to go on a safari through the wild and whimsical world of Animals and Nature. This chapter is a delightful blend of intelligence and entertainment, featuring trivia questions that reveal the funnier, less-known side of our natural world.

Into the Wild: Trivia Expedition

1. What is the loudest animal on Earth?
2. What color is a giraffe's tongue, and why?
3. Do bears really love honey?
4. Which animal produces its own sunscreen?
5. What is the only mammal that can fly?
6. What is the top speed of a cheetah?
7. What do honeybees do to communicate where food is?
8. How long have alligators been around?
9. How fast can the world's fastest snail move?
10. How long can lobsters live?
11. Which has the thickest fur of any mammal?
12. How far away can a wolf smell its prey?
13. What is the deadliest creature in the world?
14. How do dolphins sleep without drowning?
15. Which mammal is known to have the most powerful bite in the world?
16. How long is an elephant pregnant with its calf before it gives birth?
17. Which bird is unable to move their eyes?
18. Why are flamingos pink?
19. Which body part does a snake use to detect smells?
20. The nose of a lion changes color throughout its life, indicating what?
21. What animal is known to have the shortest pregnancy on Earth?
22. Where is a shrimp's heart located in its body?
23. Which animal is known to plant thousands of trees across the world?
24. On average, how many eggs can a hen lay in a year?

Animals and Nature Answers:

1. The loudest animal in the world is the **sperm whale**, which can produce a clicking sound of up to 233 decibels.
2. **Dark blue** or **black**, to protect it from sunburn.
3. **Yes**, they are attracted to the sweet substance.
4. **Hippos** secrete a red fluid that acts as sunscreen.
5. The **bat** is the only mammal that can fly.
6. Cheetahs can run **up to 75 mph**.
7. They perform a "**waggle dance.**"
8. Alligators have been around for roughly **150 million years**.
9. A Garden snail can move up to **0.03 mph**. Don't blink!
10. Lobsters can live **up to 100 years** or longer!
11. **Sea otters** have the thickest fur of any mammal, at 850,000 to one million hairs per square inch.
12. A wolf can smell its prey from **almost two miles** away.
13. The **mosquito** kills more people than any other creature in the world.
14. A dolphin only sleeps with **one half of their brain** at a time.
15. A **Hippopotamus** bite is capable of exerting about 1,800 psi.
16. An elephant is pregnant for about **22 months** before giving birth.
17. Although they can rotate their head nearly 180 degrees, **owls** cannot move their eyes.
18. Due to their main **diet mainly consisting of shrimp**, their skin takes on a pinkish color. You are what you eat!
19. A snake detects smells through its **tongue**.
20. This change in color **indicates** a lion's **age**.
21. The shortest known pregnancy is that of **an opossum**, about 12 days.
22. A shrimp's heart is located in their **head**! Wow!
23. Estimates of the number of accidental **squirrel** trees planted each

year range into the millions globally.

24. A hen can lay an average of **250-300 eggs** per year.

Prepare to continue this fascinating exploration into the realm of Food and Drink in the next chapter, where trivia meets taste buds!

6

Food and Drink - A Culinary Conundrum

Welcome to the delicious domain of Food and Drink, where culinary curiosities meet a sprinkle of humor. In this chapter, we serve up delectable trivia questions, blending important food facts with a dash of fun, to satisfy your appetite for knowledge and entertainment.

Tasty Trivia Time:

1. Where did apples originally come from?
2. Who is credited with inventing the first sandwich?
3. In which country was the first chocolate bar made?
4. What animal helped discover coffee beans?
5. How many different breeds of chicken are there?
6. What is the fastest growing plant on Earth?
7. How were potato chips invented?
8. What is currently the world's hottest chili pepper?
9. When were forks first commonly used in Western Europe?
10. What unusual ice cream flavor can be found in Japan?
11. What is a popular pizza topping in Brazil?
12. Is a banana a fruit or a herb?

13. World's Most Expensive Spice: What is it?
14. What was the original main ingredient in ketchup?
15. Who is credited with inventing champagne?
16. Why is saffron so expensive?
17. Where was tofu first created?
18. Which country consumes the most coffee per capita?
19. Oldest Recorded Recipe: What type of food was it for?
20. Why did lobsters transform from a commoner's food to a luxury item?
21. Eternal Shelf Life: Why doesn't honey spoil?
22. Where were French fries actually invented?
23. The Invention of Bubble Gum: Who invented it, and what was its original color?
24. Mushroom Mystery: Are mushrooms more closely related to plants or animals?

Food and Drink's Savory Answers:

1. Apples originated in Kazakhstan, in **central Asia** east of the Caspian Sea. By 1500 BC apple seeds had been carried throughout Europe.
2. **John Montagu**, the 4th Earl of Sandwich invented the meal that changed dining forever.
3. In **the United Kingdom**, in 1847, British chocolatier **J.S. Fry and Sons** created the first chocolate bar.
4. **Goats** helped discover coffee beans. That's why they're the G.O.A.T.
5. Over **500 breeds** of chicken.
6. **Bamboo** Is the fastest growing plant on Earth.
7. By **accident**, as a chef's spiteful response to a customer's complaint about thick fries.
8. The **Carolina Reaper** is currently the world's hottest chili pepper.
9. Forks were first commonly used during the **16th century**.
10. **Squid ink** with a mild fish taste to it.
11. A popular pizza topping in Brazil is **green peas**.
12. Botanically, it's a **berry** (thus, a fruit), but it grows from a herbaceous plant.
13. **Saffron** is known as the world's most expensive spice.
14. The first version was based on pickled **fish** and looked more like a soy sauce – with a dark and thin texture.
15. **Dom Pérignon** is credited with inventing champagne.
16. It's so expensive because Saffron is **hand-harvested** from the **crocus flower**.
17. Tofu was first discovered in **China**.
18. **Finland** consumes the most coffee per capita.
19. **Nettle pudding** dates back to 6000 BCE in Britain and is considered the oldest known recipe in the world.
20. **Over-fishing** led to its scarcity, increasing its value.
21. Honey's low moisture content **keeps bacteria from surviving**.

22. French fries were first invented in Belgium.

23. **Walter Diemer** discovered bubblegum by accident while experimenting in the lab during his breaks and the **original color** remained **pink** ever since.

24. Mushrooms are **more closely related** to **animals** due to their genetic makeup.

Next, we'll journey into the glitz and glam of Movies and Entertainment. Stay tuned for a star-studded chapter of trivia!

7

Movies and Entertainment - In The Spotlight

Step into the glamorous world of Movies and Entertainment, where behind-the-scenes curiosities and on-screen wonders blend with a touch of humor. In this chapter, we roll out the red carpet for intriguing, cinematic trivia questions, shedding light on the lesser-known aspects of the entertainment industry.

Cinema Secrets and Showbiz Trivia:

1. When did the first movie in color come out? What was it?
2. What was the world's first feature-length film?
3. Who received the first star on the Hollywood Walk of Fame?
4. What is the longest movie ever produced?
5. What was the first full-length animated movie?
6. Movie Popcorn Emergence: When did popcorn become a popular movie snack?
7. Who was the first actor to play James Bond in a movie?
8. Unusual Film Festival Location: Where is the world's most remote film festival held?
9. Disney's Mickey Mouse Original Name: What was Mickey Mouse's original name?
10. What do the Razzie Awards celebrate?
11. What was the first 3D movie released in cinemas?
12. Who holds the record for the tallest actor in Hollywood?

13. Who is credited with the invention of the movie camera?
14. What movie had the largest film set ever built?
15. What was the most expensive movie prop? And what movie was it used in?
16. The Longest TV Show Marathon: What show holds this record?
17. What is considered the first reality TV show?
18. The Most-Watched TV Series Finale: Which show holds this record?
19. What movie has spawned the most sequels?
20. The Shortest Performance to Win an Oscar: Who won and for how long were they on screen?
21. What movie first used Surround Sound?
22. Most Expensive Music Video: Which music video holds this record?
23. What is the highest-grossing film of all time?
24. What is the most filmed location in the world?

Behind the Scenes: Revealing Answers

1. The first commercially produced film in natural color was **"A Visit to the Seaside"**, and it came out in **1908**.
2. **"The Story of the Kelly Gang"** (**1906**) was the first feature-length film
3. **Joanne Woodward** received the first star on the Hollywood Walk of Fame.
4. **"Logistics,"** running for **35 days and 17 hours** was the longest movie ever produced.
5. "**Snow White and the Seven Dwarfs**" (**1937**) was the first full-length animated movie.
6. Popcorn became a popular movie snack **during the Great Depression** in the **1930**s.
7. **Sean Connery** was the first actor to play James Bond in a movie.
8. The world's most remote film festival is held in **Antarctica**.
9. **Mortimer Mouse** was Mickey Mouse's original name.
10. The **worst** cinematic achievements.
11. "**Bwana Devil**" (**1952**) was the first 3D movie released in cinemas.
12. **Brad Garrett**, standing at 6 feet 8 inches tall, holds the record for the tallest actor in Hollywood.
13. **Thomas Edison** and **William Kennedy Laurie Dickson** invented the movie camera.
14. "**Cleopatra**" (**1963**) held the largest film set ever built.
15. The **Maltese Falcon** from "The Maltese Falcon," valued at over $4 million was the most expensive movie prop ever used!
16. **"The Simpsons,"** with a marathon of 13 days.
17. **"An American Family"** (**1973**) was considered the first "reality" show.
18. "**MAS*H**" in **1983** holds the record for the most watched finale episode.

19. **"Godzilla,"** with over 30 sequels.
20. **Beatrice Straight** in "Network" for **5 minutes and 40 seconds**.
21. **"Apocalypse Now"** (1979) was the first movie to use Surround Sound.
22. Michael Jackson's **"Scream"** holds the record for the most expensive music video.
23. **"Avatar"**, is currently the highest-grossing film of all time.
24. **Central Park** in **New York City** is the most filmed location in the world.

Prepare for an encore as we switch gears to Music Trivia!

8

Musical History and Lore

Welcome to the melodious world of Music, where every note tells a story and every rhythm hides a fun fact. In this chapter, we tune into trivia questions exploring the quirky corners and high notes of music.

Tuneful Trivia:

1. Oldest Known Musical Instrument: What is it and how old is it?
2. The Beatles' Original Name: What was The Beatles' first band name?
3. Which classical composer was deaf?
4. What is the fear of music called?
5. Mozart's Quirky Talent: What unique ability did Mozart have regarding music?
6. The World's Most Covered Song: Which song holds this title?
7. Who was the first woman inducted into the Rock and Roll Hall of Fame?
8. Which country has the shortest national anthem?
9. Who sang the Spongebob Squarepants theme song for the movie?
10. Where and when was karaoke invented?
11. Most Expensive Musical Instrument: What is it?
12. Music and Plants: How does classical music affect plant growth?
13. Where and when did rap music start?
14. What is unique about the Ice Music Festival?
15. The Longest Guitar Solo: Who played it and how long was it?
16. What is often considered the first rock and roll song?
17. The Invention of the Piano: Who invented it and in what year?
18. The Most Streamed Song on Spotify: What is it?
19. What was the shortest song to win a Grammy?
20. How does music affect cow milk production?
21. Where did disco music originate?
22. What is considered the first country music song?

Symphonic Solutions: Musical Answers

1. A **flute** made from bird bone, approximately **35,000 years old**.
2. John Lennon assembled his skiffle group, first calling it the **Black Jacks**, and then the **QuarryMen**. The group went through several name changes.
3. **Ludwig Van Beethoven** began to lose hearing at age 28, and was completely deaf by the age of 44.
4. **Melophobia** is the fear of music. Woah!
5. He could **write music perfectly from memory**.
6. **"Yesterday"** by **The Beatles** remains popular today with more than 1,600 recorded cover versions.
7. **Aretha Franklin** was the first woman inducted into the Rock and Roll Hall of Fame on Jan. 3, **1987**..
8. As well as being one of the oldest known national anthems, **Japan**

also has the world's shortest national anthem, standing at just a single verse.

9. In the movie, Avril Lavigne sang the soundtrack for Spongebob Squarepants.

10. Karaoke is well-known nowadays, but it started in **Kobe, Japan** around **1971**.

11. The most expensive instrument in the world is occupied by the "**MacDonald**" **Stradivarius viola**, which is valued at over **45 million** dollars. Wow!

12. It can **speed up** a plant's **growth**.

13. **In the Bronx**, New York City, in the **1970s** was considered the birth of rap music.

14. It's held **in an igloo** and features **instruments made of ice**.

15. **David DiDonato** held the record for the longest guitar solo, lasting 24 hours and 55 minutes.

16. "**Rock Around the Clock**" by Bill Haley & His Comets is often considered the first rock and roll song.

17. The piano was invented by **Bartolomeo Cristofori** in the **early 18th century**.

18. "**Shape of You**" by **Ed Sheeran**, currently is the most streamed song on Spotify.

19. The shortest winner, Henry Mancini's melancholy "**Days Of Wine And Roses**" (1963), clocks in at **2 minutes and 5 seconds**.

20. Music's effect on cows can actually **increase milk production**. Crazy!

21. Disco music originated in **the United States** in the **1970s**.

22. "**Sallie Gooden**" by Fiddlin' John Carson is considered the first country music song.

Next up, we're dialing back the clock to explore the captivating world of World History. Stay tuned for a journey through time!

9

World History - Time-Traveling Trivia

Take a ride on this historical odyssey with a twist! This chapter is a time capsule of engaging and humorous trivia questions about World History. From ancient empires to historical facts, we journey through time, uncovering the lesser-known, yet fascinating aspects of our past.

Historical Hilarity Trivia:

1. The Shortest War in History: Which countries fought in it, and how long did it last?
2. The First Recorded "UFO" Sighting: When and where did it happen?
3. What was the original color of carrots?
4. What was it originally named before being named New York?
5. When and where was paper invented?
6. When was bubble wrap invented? What was its original intended use?
7. When and where were the oldest recorded "Yo Mama" jokes ever found?
8. Who wore the tallest hat in history and how tall was it?
9. In which ocean did the Titanic sink? And when?
10. Where is the oldest University and when was it founded?
11. Which civilization first discovered chocolate?
12. What other job did Abraham Lincoln have?
13. Historical Figure's Phobia: What was Julius Caesar afraid of?
14. The First Parachute Jump: When and from what height was it made?
15. What unusual dental practice did the Ancient Romans have?
16. What was the first novel ever written and who wrote it?
17. Who became the first man to fly solo and non-stop across the Atlantic?
18. The First Item Bought Online: What was it and when?
19. Who received the first ever speeding ticket? And for how fast?
20. How many U.S. presidents have been assassinated, and who were they?
21. Which mountaineer and his Sherpa became the first men to conquer Mount Everest? And when?
22. Which attack by the Japanese navy caused the U.S. to declare war on Japan and enter World War 2?

23. Which was the last of the 50 U.S. states to join the union?

Timeless Tidbits: Historical Answers

1. **Britain** and **Zanzibar** once fought a war lasting only **38 minutes**.
2. **Nuremberg, Germany**, in **1561** was the first recorded "UFO" sighting.
3. The original color of carrots was actually **purple**.
4. Before it got its current name, New York used to be named **New Amsterdam**.
5. Dunder Mifflin Paper Company, Inc. Just kidding, it was actually invented in **China, around 100 BC.**
6. Created in **1957**, the original intended use of bubble wrap was as **wallpaper**. Woah!

7. Around **1,500 BCE**, a student in **ancient Babylon** inscribed six riddles on a tablet.

8. **Abraham Lincoln**'s stovepipe hat was the tallest, standing about **7 inches tall**.

9. On **April 15, 1912**, the Titanic sank in the **North Atlantic Ocean**.

10. The University of **Al Quaraouiyine** in Morocco, founded in **859**.

11. **The Olmec**, one of the earliest civilizations in Latin America, were the first to turn the cacao plant into chocolate.

12. Abraham Lincoln was also a **licensed bartender**. Serving up drinks!

13. You wouldn't believe it, Julius Caesar was **afraid of cats**!

14. In **1797**, from approximately **3,200 feet**.

15. The Ancient Romans used **urine** as **mouthwash**. Ew!

16. "**The Tale of Genji**" was the first novel written by **Murasaki Shikibu**.

17. In 1927, **Charles Lindbergh** became the first man to fly solo and non-stop across the Atlantic

18. The first item ever bought online was a **Sting CD**, in **1994**.

19. It was a motorist in **1896**, going **8 mph**.

20. There were **four** presidents assassinated: **Abraham Lincoln**, **James A. Garfield**, **William McKinley**, **John F. Kennedy**.

21. On May 29, **1953**, **Sir Edmund Hillary** and **Tenzing Norgay** became the first men to conquer Mount Everest.

22. On December 7, 1941, the **Japanese attack on Pearl Harbor** caused the United States to declare war on Japan and enter World War 2.

23. **Hawaii** was the last of the 50 U.S. states to join the union on **August 21, 1959**.

Next, we'll raise our glasses to a chapter filled with Holiday and Tradition trivia. Prepare for a festive dive into celebrations around the globe!

10

Holidays and Traditions - A Festive Adventure

Enjoy a whimsical journey through the world of Holidays and Traditions. This chapter is your ticket to exploring trivia questions that delve into the delights of global festivities and customs.

Holiday and Heritage Trivia:

1. What is an unusual New Year's tradition in Spain?
2. What was Santa's original suit color?
3. What is Mardi Gras and its origin?
4. Halloween's Original Vegetable: What was originally carved instead of pumpkins?
5. The Largest Easter Egg Ever Made: How big was it?

6. Thanksgiving's Different Date: Which country celebrates Thanksgiving in October?
7. What do families traditionally eat on Thanksgiving?
8. The Invention of Fireworks: Where and when were they invented?
9. Easter Island's Name Origin: Why is it called Easter Island?
10. What is the world's oldest holiday and where did it originate?
11. Leap Year's Unique Tradition in Ireland: What is encouraged for women?
12. Which country holds the oldest Independence Day celebration?
13. What do the Russians write and burn for their New Year Tradition?
14. What is Hanukkah and who celebrates it?
15. Who gifted the United States the Statue of Liberty? And when?
16. The Origin of Mother's Day: Where and when was it first celebrated?
17. What color was originally associated with St. Patrick's Day?
18. What do men traditionally do for Father's Day in Germany?
19. What unusual race is held on Australia Day?
20. The Origin of Valentine's Hearts: Why are they shaped that way?
21. Chinese New Year's Superstition: What should you not do on this day?
22. The Most Fireworks: Which country holds the record for the most fireworks?
23. Why do people kiss under the Mistletoe?
24. What was the tallest Christmas tree ever recorded?

Celebratory Chronicles: Enlightening Answers

1. People in Spain **eat grapes** for good luck **at** each stroke of **midnight**.
2. Prior to Nast's work, Santa's outfit was **tan** in color, and it was he that changed it to red, although he also drew Santa in a **green suit**.
3. Mardi Gras was initially celebrated as a way to mark the **beginning of Lent** and to **prepare for** the fasting period of **Easter**.
4. **Turnips** were originally carved instead of pumpkins for Halloween.
5. The largest decorated Easter egg is around **54 feet** and **10 inches** tall..
6. **Canada** celebrates Thanksgiving on the second Monday in October.
7. Traditional foods include **turkey**, **stuffing**, **gravy**, **sweet potatoes**, **mashed potatoes**, and **cranberry sauce**. Many people also serve **pie** for dessert.
8. Fireworks were invented **in China**, around the **7th century**.
9. Because 'Easter Island' was **discovered** on **Easter Sunday** in **1722**.
10. The world's oldest holiday is **New Year's Day**, from ancient Babylon.

Earliest record of festivities celebrating the arrival of the new year was around **2000 BCE**.

11. As part of the leap year Irish tradition known as Bachelor's Day, women are permitted to **make marriage proposals to males**.

12. **Denmark** has the oldest Independence day dating back to 1912.

13. The Russians write and burn **their wishes**, then drink the ashes in champagne for their New Year's tradition.

14. Hanukkah is a **Jewish festival** that **celebrates freedom from oppression** by the lighting of candles on each day of the festival.

15. On **July 4, 1884**, **France** presented the United States with an incredible birthday gift: the Statue of Liberty!

16. In the **United States**, **1908** was the origin of Mother's Day.

17. The earliest depictions of St. Patrick shows him clothed in **blue** garments, not green.

18. **Going hiking** and **drinking beer** is a normal Father's Day tradition in Germany.

19. A **cockroach race** is held on Australia Day. Gross!

20. It's an **old depiction to represent the human heart**. They were a little off!

21. You **should not be sweeping**, to not sweep away good luck!

22. The country that holds the record for the most fireworks is **China**

23. Ancient **fertility rites** and the belief in the Mistletoe's **healing power**.

24. The world's tallest-ever Christmas Tree stood in a shopping center in Seattle at a whopping **221 feet**. Amazing!

Up next, we gear up for some brain-teasing excitement in the chapter on Puzzles and Brain Teasers. Get ready for a mind-bending adventure!

11

Riddles and Brain Teasers - The Mental Gymnasium

Welcome to the mental workout room where your brain gets to flex its muscles! In this chapter, we present intriguing riddles and brain teasers, designed to challenge, entertain, and enlighten.

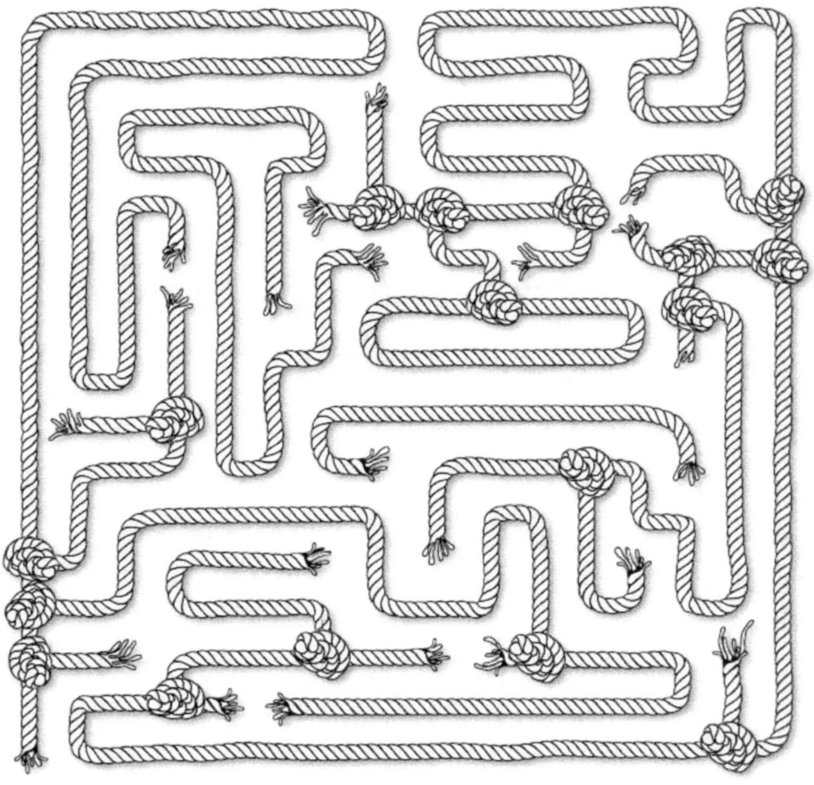

Cerebral Challenges: Mind-Bending Mysteries

1. What has a face and two hands but no arms or legs?
2. Why are ghosts bad at lying?
3. What is always in front of you but can't be seen?
4. What has to be broken before you can use it?
5. What happened in 1961 and will not happen again until 6009?
6. What has a head and a tail but no body?
7. What's the longest word in the English language?
8. In baseball, how many outs are there in an inning?

9. What word when written in capital letters is the same backward, frontward, and upside down?

10. What two words when combined hold the most letters?

11. Do you know the name of the invention that lets you look instantly right through any wall you want?

12. What is something you can serve but shouldn't ever eat?

13. Do you know where you can find cities and countries, towns and shops, roads and lakes, but absolutely no people whatsoever?

14. There's a question that you can never answer yes to. Do you know what it is?

15. I am an odd number, but if you take away just a single letter, I become even. Can you guess my number?

16. I am a ball that can be rolled but never bounced or thrown. What am I?

17. How can a man go 8 days without sleep?

18. Can you name three consecutive days without using the words Wednesday, Friday, and Sunday?

19. What occurs once in a minute, twice in a moment, and never in one thousand years?

20. If you are running in a race and you pass the person in second place, what place are you in?

21. How many months have 28 days?

22. What element is not on the periodic table?

23. When things go wrong, what can you always count on?

Enlightening Riddle Explanations:

1. A **clock**
2. Because **you can see right through them**.
3. The **future**
4. An **egg**
5. The year will again be the same **upside down**
6. A **coin**
7. **Smiles.** Because there's a mile between the beginning and the end.
8. **Six.** Each team has three.
9. **NOON**
10. **Post Office**
11. A **window**
12. A **volleyball**
13. A **map**
14. Are you **asleep** yet?
15. **Seven**
16. An **eyeball**

17. He only sleeps **at night**.
18. **Yesterday**, **today**, and **tomorrow**
19. The letter **M**
20. **Second Place**
21. All **12** months!
22. The element of **surprise**!
23. Your **fingers** and **toes**, haha!

Get ready to move from mental puzzles to bizarre and unusual facts in our next chapter, where things get even more curious!

12

Bizarre and Unusual Facts - The Oddity Odyssey

Discover an array of strange and unexpected turns in this chapter, where we unveil bizarre and unusual trivia questions and facts. These are not your everyday tidbits; they're a collection of the most peculiar, intriguing, and downright weird aspects of the world.

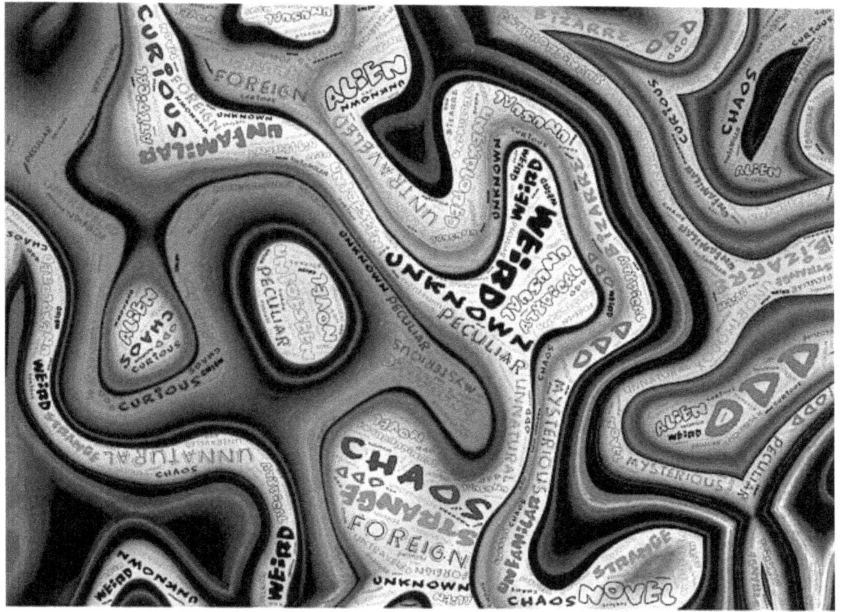

Weird and Wonderful Wonders of Trivia:

1. Which famous product was originally marketed as the "Esteemed Brain Tonic and Intellectual Beverage"?
2. What common American federal crime do many Netflix streamers commit, perhaps by accident?
3. Though smoking is illegal on flights, what piece of smoking paraphernalia must be kept on every plane in case of an emergency?
4. What do the two "M"s of M&Ms stand for?
5. Who holds the unfortunate Guinness World Record of most bones broken?
6. What is the least popular car color internationally?
7. The world's largest tire manufacturing company is, surprisingly, what?
8. How many liters of saliva does the average human produce in their

lifetime?

9. Why do plastic water bottles have expiration dates?

10. What unassuming barnyard animal has the closest genetic resemblance to the long extinct Tyrannosaurus Rex?

11. What type of apparel is exempt from taxation in Texas?

12. Approximately how many different customized drinks are possible at Starbucks?

13. Students at Purdue University engineered a "licking machine" to find out once and for all how many licks it takes to get to the center of a Tootsie Pop. How many licks did they conclude it took?

14. What did the first webcam ever stream at the University of Cambridge in 1993?

15. What everyday item was originally called the "Whirlwind" before its name was changed?

16. What percentage of the world is allergic to cats?

17. How much does the largest rubber band ball weigh?

18. When was the first recorded use of "OMG" standing for "Oh My God"?

19. How many people participated in the world's largest pillow fight?

20. What can quickly increase the amount of bacteria in your ears?

21. What is the only part of the human body that can't heal itself?

22. What event used to be part of the Olympics that is no longer today?

23. What did Americans use to wipe before we invented toilet paper?

Answers: Unraveling the Unusual

1. Believe it or not, **Coca-Cola** was originally marketed as the "Esteemed Brain Tonic and Intellectual Beverage".
2. Watching movies and television from a **friend's Netflix account**. Oh snap!
3. An **ashtray** must be kept on every plane in case of an emergency.
4. The names of the candy's creators: Forrest **Mars** and Bruce **Murrie**
5. The record for the most broken bones in a lifetime is held by **Evel Knievel** who sustained **433 fractures.**
6. **Purple** is the least popular car color internationally.
7. **LEGO** is the world's largest tire manufacturing company and produces more tires annually than any other company.
8. The average human produces approximately **40,000 liters** of saliva

in their lifetime.

9. The water doesn't expire, but the **plastic will** start to break down and **contaminate** the **water** if consumed past the expiration date.
10. The **chicken**, crazy!
11. **Cowboy boots** are not taxed in Texas. Wild!
12. About **87,000** different drinks can be made at Starbucks! Wow!
13. The world may never know! Just kidding, it was **364 licks**.
14. A **coffee pot** – so people could check if it was empty or full. Talk about convenience!
15. The **vacuum cleaner**. Whirlwind sounds cooler.
16. Approximately **10%** of the world is allergic. How cat-a-strophic.
17. The rubber band ball weighs over **9,000 pounds** and towers at about **6 feet** and **7 inches** tall.
18. The first documented use of "OMG" was **in 1917** in a letter to none other than Winston Churchill.
19. **7,681 people** participated in a pillow fight in Minneapolis, Minnesota in 2018. Imagine the feathers!
20. **Wearing headphones** for just an hour could increase the bacteria in your ears by about **700 times**. Ew!
21. Our **teeth** are not made of live tissue and are coated in enamel, which can't spontaneously regenerate.
22. Competitive **Art**! From 1912 to 1948, artists could earn medals for **painting**, **music**, **sculpture**, and even **architecture**.
23. Early North American settlers used **corn cobs** before we had toilet paper. They were abundant, they were soft and they were easy to handle.

Next, we journey into the realm of Science Fiction and Fantasy, where imagination meets the incredible. Get ready for an adventure into the extraordinary!

13

Sci-Fi and Fantasy - Journey into Imagination

Step into a realm where fantasy becomes possible and the boundaries of reality are stretched. In this chapter, we delve into trivia questions about science fiction and fantasy, exploring the iconic and awe-inspiring elements of these imaginative genres.

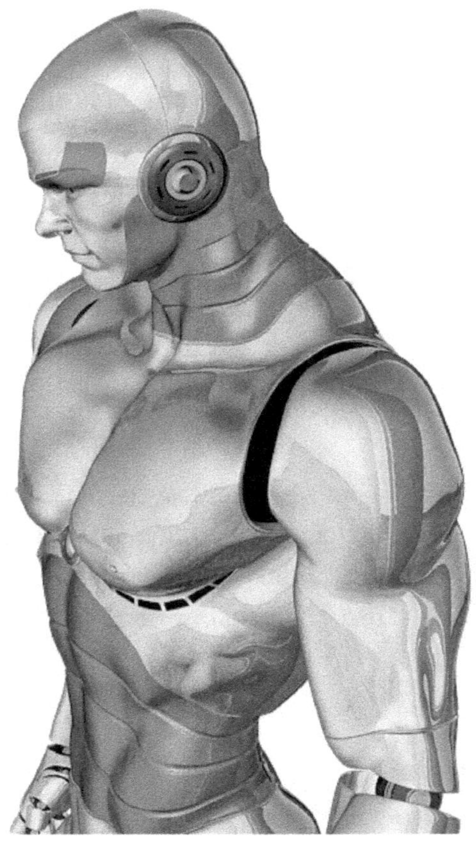

Mystical Questions: Sci-Fi and Fantasy Facts Unearthed

1. What is considered the first science fiction novel?
2. The Creator of Middle-Earth: Who invented the Elvish language?
3. What was the first science fiction film ever made?
4. What was the original Godzilla suit made from?
5. Which fantasy series took the longest to complete?
6. Where did the term 'Robot' originate?
7. What is the name of the American animated sci-fi sitcom about the

misadventures of a mad scientist and his grandson?

8. Who is considered the first superhero in comics?

9. In the 'Star Wars' universe, what was the color of Master Yoda's lightsaber?

10. In the TV series "Stranger Things", what is the name of the parallel dimension?

11. Who played the lead role of Neo in "The Matrix" trilogy?

12. Which character spoke the very first line in the original 1977 Star Wars movie?

13. Who directed the movie "E.T. the Extra-Terrestrial"?

14. In what 1984 movie does an actor play a cyborg assassin sent back in time to kill a future resistance leader? Who was the actor?

15. What is the name of the main character in the book and movie The Hunger Games?

16. What is the name of the planet that the Na'vi live on in the movie "Avatar"?

17. In which 1985 movie does Michael J. Fox travel back in time to the 1950s in a DeLorean time machine?

18. What was the first fantasy novel to win a Pulitzer Prize?

19. In what 1997 movie did actors play secret agents tasked with policing extraterrestrial life on Earth? Who were the actors?

20. What movie is about a paleontologist touring an almost complete theme park on an island in Central America is tasked with protecting kids after a power failure causes the park's cloned dinosaurs to run loose?

21. Which fictional character has been adapted or portrayed the most in film?

22. Where did Harry Potter originate from? And from who?

23. How did Marvel originate?

Answers: Exploring the Unknown

1. **"Frankenstein"** published in 1818 by Mary Shelley is considered the first science fiction novel.
2. **J.R.R. Tolkien** created his Elvish languages using a combination of his knowledge of historical linguistics, his love of poetry and myth, and his imagination.
3. **"A Trip to the Moon"** (1902) was widely considered to be the first ever sci-fi film.
4. The monster suit trivas made out of primitive materials including **heavy urethane** (latex) and **bamboo**.
5. **"The Wheel of Time"** by Robert Jordan is one of the longest fantasy series out there including 15 books, 4.4 million-odd words and 147

unique points of view. That's a lot!

6. The word itself derives from the Czech word "robota," or **forced labor**.

7. **Rick and Morty**

8. Created by Lee Falk, the first superhero was **The Phantom**, who debuted in his own newspaper comic strip on 17 Feb **1936**.

9. Yoda's lightsaber is **green**.

10. **The Upside Down** was the name of the parallel universe in "Stranger Things".

11. The character of Neo was played by **Keanu Reeves** in the hit movie series!

12. The first line ever spoken in the 'Star Wars' series was by **C-3PO**.

13. "E.T." was directed by **Steven Spielberg**.

14. **Arnold Schwarzenegger** is featured in **"The Terminator"**.

15. The main character is named **Katniss Everdeen**.

16. The planet that the Na'vi live on is called **Pandora**.

17. This movie about time travel is called **"Back to the Future"**.

18. **"The Amazing Adventures of Kavalier & Clay"** by Michael Chabon.

19. The movie is called **"Men In Black"** and the actors were **Will Smith and Tommy Lee Jones**.

20. This 1993 film directed by Steven Spielberg is called **"Jurassic Park"** which is a depiction of the 1990 science fiction novel written by Michael Crichton.

21. **Sherlock Holmes** is the most portrayed character from fiction, with over 254 movies and TV shows.

22. **J.K. Rowling** had the idea for Harry Potter while delayed on a train traveling from Manchester to London King's Cross in 1990. Go figure!

23. Timely Comics, the precursor to Marvel Comics, was **founded in 1939** by pulp magazine publisher **Martin Goodman**.

As we close this chapter, we prepare to navigate the intriguing landscapes of World Geography in our next section. Join us for a voyage across continents and cultures!

14

World Geography - Global Trivia

Enjoy a geographical journey like no other! This chapter brings you fascinating trivia questions about World Geography. From different landmarks to the most peculiar natural phenomena, we traverse the globe uncovering intelligent, humorous, and entertaining facts about our world.

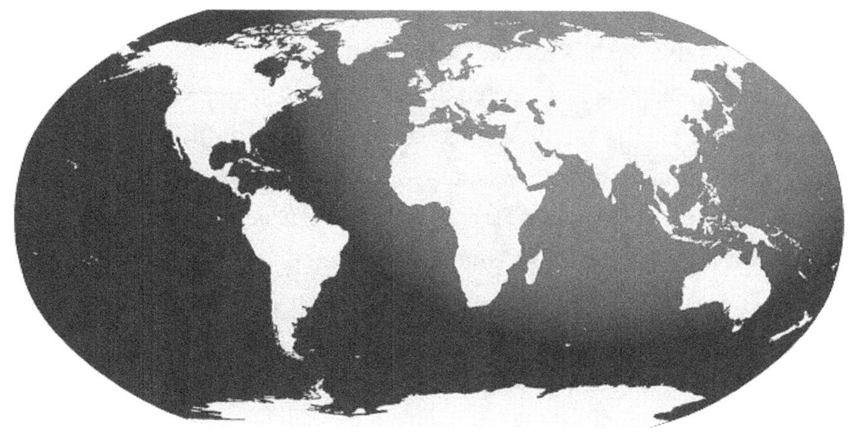

Globetrotting Guesswork: Unlocking Earth's Secrets

1. Which country has the most time zones?
2. Which famous river flows north?
3. Which country is a mosquito-free zone?
4. World's Smallest Country: What is it and how big is it?
5. What is the name of the super continent that existed 200 million years ago?
6. In what ocean is the Bermuda Triangle located?
7. Which country holds the record for the most volcanoes?
8. What is the name of the deepest point in Earth's oceans?
9. What is the world's oldest national park?
10. What is the largest desert on the planet?
11. Where is a city with a population of one?
12. Which country has the most natural lakes in it?
13. What is the name of the shortest river and where is it located?
14. Which country has the most official languages and how many languages are there?
15. Which country has more bikes than people?
16. What is the world's longest mountain range?
17. Where is there a city located under a rock?
18. How long is the world's shortest commercial flight?
19. Which country has a town named 'Batman'?
20. Where can you find a waterfall taller than a skyscraper?
21. What is the largest man-made structure?

Answers: Discovering Earth's Oddities

1. **France**, including its overseas territories, has the most time zones with **12**.
2. **The Nile River** flows north.
3. **Iceland** is the only nation with no mosquitoes. Lucky!
4. **Vatican City** spanning a whopping **0.17** square miles!
5. All of the continents we know of today existed as a single continent called **Pangea**.
6. The Bermuda Triangle is a region in the western part of the North **Atlantic Ocean**.
7. **Indonesia** has the most volcanoes of any country in the world, with **76 volcanoes** that have erupted at least **1,171 times** in **total** within historical times.
8. **Mariana's Trench** was estimated to go all the way down to **35,814** feet!
9. **Yellowstone National Park**, USA is the oldest national park estab-

lished in 1872.

10. The largest desert on the planet is the **Antarctic Polar Desert**.

11. **Monowi, Nebraska** garnered national and international recognition after the 2010 United States census counted **only one resident** of the village.

12. **Canada** has the most natural lakes in the world. About **9%** of Canada's surface area is covered by lakes.

13. The **Roe River**, Montana, USA is **only 201 feet long** at its longest constant point.

14. **Zimbabwe** has the most with 16 different languages.

15. The **Netherlands** has more bikes than citizens, and even the country's prime minister often cycles to work.

16. The **Andes mountains** is the world's longest mountain range.

17. **Setenil de las Bodegas in Spain** brings a whole new meaning to the term "living under a rock".

18. Approximately **two minutes**, in Scotland's Orkney Islands.

19. Batman is a town in **southeastern Turkey**, in the center of the country's oil-producing region.

20. **Angel Falls**, **Venezuela**. The world's tallest waterfall stands more than a **half mile high** in Venezuela's Canaima National Park.

21. The **Great Wall of China** is the largest man-made structure having a length of 13,171 miles.

Next, we prepare to delve into the realm of Health and Medicine, where science meets the human body in fascinating ways. Stay tuned for insights and curiosities in health and wellness!

15

Health and Medicine - A Dose of Knowledge

Welcome to a unique exploration of Health and Medicine, where facts are stranger than fiction, and learning can be as entertaining as it is enlightening. In this chapter, we dive into trivia questions that unveil the bizarre and fascinating aspects of health and medicine from around the world.

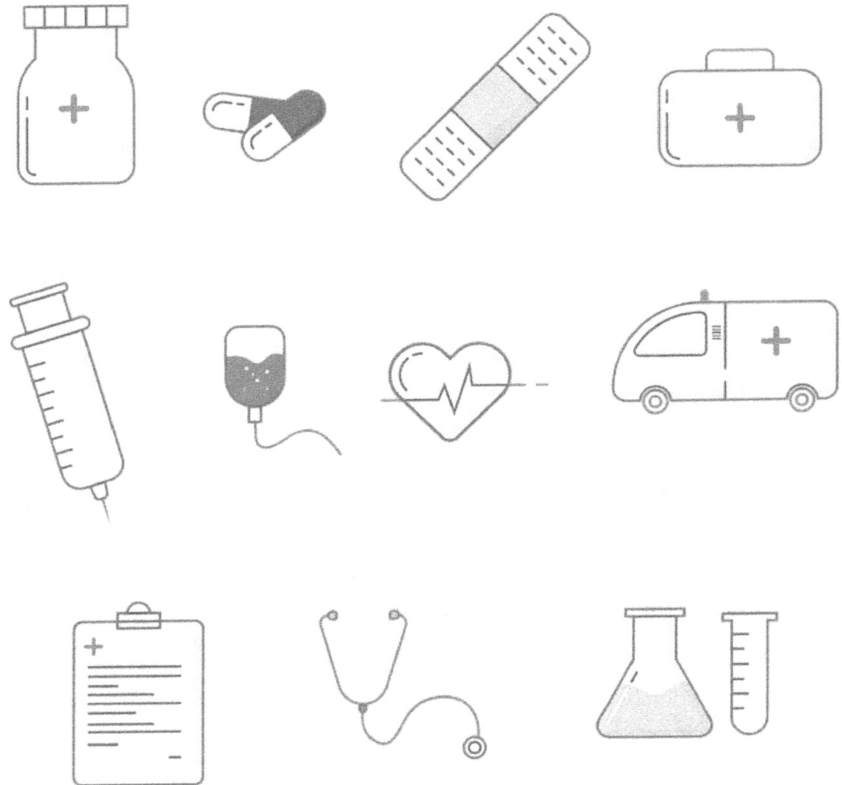

Curative Curiosities: Medical Marvels Uncovered

1. What is the human body's strongest muscle?
2. What unusual thing was once prescribed as medicine?
3. The First Organ Transplant: What organ was it and when?
4. What is the oldest medical procedure in the world?
5. What is the oldest medicine still used today?
6. What was the first ever plastic surgery? And when was it?
7. Are identical twins fingerprints the same?
8. What is the rarest blood type in humans?

9. What is the largest human organ in the body?
10. How much DNA do humans share with chimpanzees?
11. When was the first test tube baby born?
12. How many taste buds does a normal healthy human have?
13. What are leeches used for in modern medicine?
14. How long did the longest hiccups last?
15. Who discovered X-Rays? And when?
16. What was the reason behind the invention of Band-Aids? And when were they first made?
17. Which country has the highest life expectancy in the world?
18. What percentage of the human body is water?
19. Which body part continues to grow throughout a person's life?
20. What healthy compound does chocolate contain?
21. When were glasses invented and where?

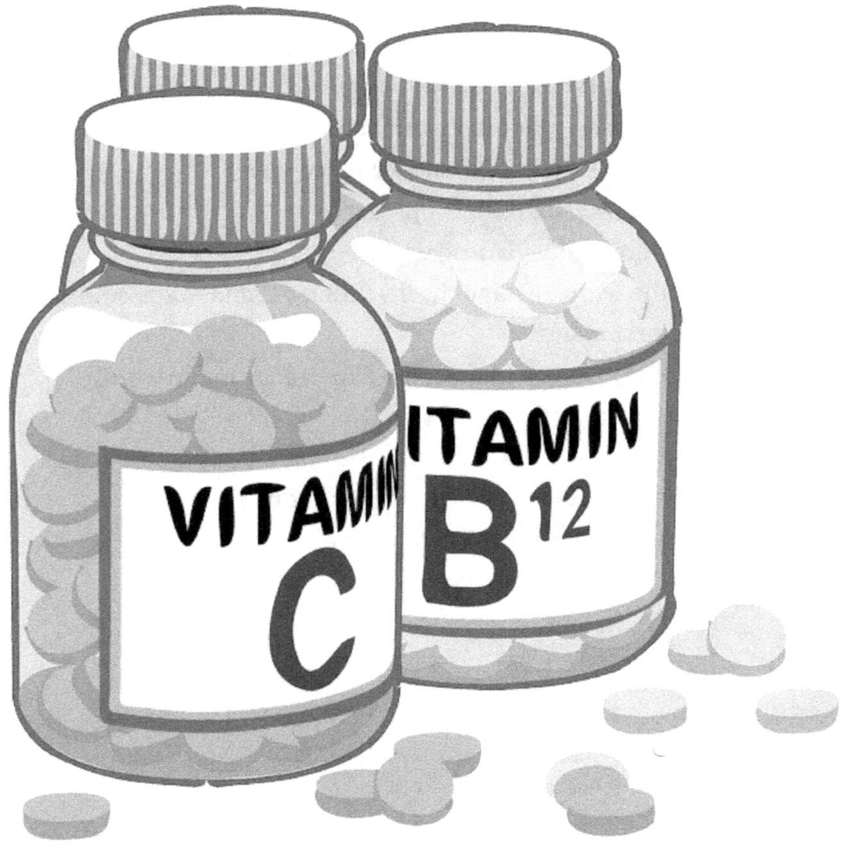

Answers: Healing and History

1. The strongest muscle in the human body is the **masseter muscle** in the **jaw**.
2. The medicinal use of cacao, or **chocolate**, both as a primary remedy and to deliver other medicines as well.
3. The **kidney** was the first human organ to be transplanted success-fully **in 1954**.
4. Humanity's oldest form of surgery is **trepanation**—the practice of

drilling holes in the skull as a means of curing illnesses.

5. The **bark of the willow tree** contains one of the oldest medicinal remedies for **pain relief** in human history. In its modern form, we call it **aspirin**.

6. Physicians in ancient India used **skin grafts** for reconstructive surgery as early as **800 B.C.**

7. **No**, like those who aren't twins, identical twins all have unique fingerprints.

8. **AB negative** is the rarest of the eight main blood types - just 1% of our donors have it.

9. The **skin** is the largest organ of the human body.

10. Humans and chimps share a surprising **98.8 percent** of their DNA.

11. The birth of the world's first 'test-tube baby', Louise Brown, on **July 25th, 1978** in Oldham, northwest England.

12. The average adult can have up to **10,000** taste buds, but you lose them as you grow older. Wow!

13. Leeches are excellent at **promoting circulation of blood** in a specific area.

14. American Charles Osborne had hiccups for **68 years**, from 1922 to 1990. Oh my!

15. **Wilhelm Conrad Röntgen** reported the discovery of X-rays in **December 1895**.

16. The Band-Aid was invented in **1920** by a Johnson & Johnson employee, Earle Dickson, **for his wife**, who frequently cut and burned herself while cooking.

17. **Monaco**, near France, has the highest life expectancy in the world in 2023, according to World Population Review, where locals live to an average age of 87.

18. In adults, about **60%** of their body is made of water.

19. While the rest of our body shrinks as we get older, our **noses, earlobes** and **ear muscles** keep getting bigger.

20. Most dark chocolate is rich in plant chemicals called **flavanols**. Flavanols are antioxidants linked to a **lower risk of heart disease**. Win for chocolate lovers!
21. One of the first recorded pair of glasses were made in **1284** by Salvino D'Armate **in Italy**.

As we close this enlightening chapter on Health and Medicine, we prepare to embark on a literary adventure in Arts and Literature. Prepare to explore the creative expressions of humanity through time!

16

Arts and Literature - A Canvas of Curiosities

Dive into the vibrant world of Arts and Literature with this chapter, where we explore engaging trivia questions. These questions span a range of topics, from fun facts about famous artists and literary figures to peculiar moments in art and literary history.

Artistic and Literary Amusements:

1. What common facial feature is absent in the Mona Lisa?

2. Who was Edgar Allan Poe's wife and how were they related?

3. What was unique about how J.K. Rowling wrote the first 'Harry Potter' manuscript?

4. A young boy takes a train to the North Pole on Christmas Eve in what classic 1985 children's book by Chris Van Allsburg? (hint: also a movie)

5. What is often considered the first modern novel?

6. In the classic 1957 children's book, "How the Grinch Stole Christmas," what is the name of the town the Grinch steals presents and decorations from?

7. What is the priciest piece of art on the planet?

8. Where does the Wizard live in The Wizard of Oz?

9. The five categories in which Nobel Prizes are awarded are Peace, Chemistry, Literature, Physiology/Medicine, and what?

10. How many times did the famous author, Emily Dickinson, leave her home in adulthood?

11. The First Detective Novel: What is it and who wrote it?

12. What is the largest painting ever created?

13. How many paintings did Van Gogh sell during his lifetime?

14. What event inspired the sky in "The Scream", a famous painting?

15. What was Bram Stoker's initial name for Dracula?

16. Ernest Hemingway's Standing Desk: Why did he write standing up?

17. What is the name of Herman Melville's famous book about a whale?

18. What book has sold the most copies of all time?

19. What is the oldest known story and where does it originate from?

20. What was the name of the theater where many of Shakespeare's plays were performed?

21. What is the oldest known form of artwork to date?

Artistic Answers: Unveiling the Unusual

1. One long-standing mystery of the painting is why Mona Lisa features no **eyebrows** and apparently does not have any **eyelashes**.

2. The couple were **first cousins** and publicly married when Virginia

Clemm was 13 and Poe was 27.

3. J.K. Rowling **wrote** the first book **on scraps of toilet paper**. Wow!

4. The book is called **The Polar Express**.

5. On January 16, 1605, **Don Quixote** written by Miguel de Cervantes is widely considered to be the first modern novel.

6. The town of **Whoville** is where he ravages gifts from the children.

7. The most expensive painting ever sold is the **Salvator Mundi** painted by Leonardo da Vinci in the 1500s and sold for **$450.3 million** in 2017.

8. The wizard lives in **Emerald City**.

9. The final category missing is **Physics**.

10. Believe it or not, she left her home **only one** time during adulthood! Dedication!

11. **"Murders in the Rue Morgue,"** Edgar Allan Poe's detective story, was published in **1841.**

12. Emad Salehi has the largest art canvas measuring at around 103,893 square ft. in Doha, Qatar called "**The story of the ball**". **19 times as big** as a basketball court!

13. Van Gogh only sold **one** painting during his lifetime. The rest of his more than 900 paintings were not sold or made famous until after his death.

14. The dramatic red-colored sky was inspired by a volcanic sunset seen by Munch after the Krakatau **volcano eruption** in 1883.

15. Coming across the name Dracula in his reading on Romanian history, he chose this to replace the name **Count Wampyr** that he had originally planned to use for his villain.

16. Ernest Hemingway almost always stood to work, due to a **leg injury** from World War I.

17. **Moby Dick** was published in London in October **1851** as The Whale and a month later in New York City as Moby Dick.

18. **The Bible** is the best selling book of all time with over an estimated

5 billion copies sold and distributed.

19. The oldest surviving literary work is **The Epic of Gilgamesh**. It was composed nearly **4,000 years ago** in ancient **Mesopotamia** (near the Middle East).

20. **The Globe**, which opened in **1599**, became the playhouse where audiences first saw some of Shakespeare's best-known plays.

21. The world's oldest-known artwork is three wild pigs painted deep **in a limestone cave** on the Indonesian island of Sulawesi at least **45,500 years ago**.

As we turn the page from the intriguing world of Arts and Literature, we set our sights on the thrilling domain of Travel and Adventure in the next chapter. Get ready to embark on a journey of discovery!

17

All Aboard! - Traveling and Adventure

Pack your bags and lace up your boots! In this chapter, we explore trivia questions about Traveling and Adventure. From the world's most exotic destinations to historical explorations, we span the globe in search of the most fascinating travel facts.

Journeys, Travels, and Trivia:

1. What is the world's most visited city?
2. Approximately how many airplane flights depart and land every day?
3. What is the largest city and what is the population?
4. On what Caribbean Island can you swim with pigs?
5. Who holds the world's largest food fight, and what food is thrown?
6. What is the world's oldest city and where is it located?
7. What countries share the world's longest international border?
8. What country has the largest pyramid (by volume) in the world?
9. What country is obsessed with eating Kentucky Fried Chicken (K.F.C.) on Christmas Day?
10. What is the busiest airport in the world?

11. What is the highest point in the world?

12. Known as "The Big Easy," what is the actual name of this southern American city?

13. Where is the world's oldest operating airport?

14. Notre Dame, a famous medieval cathedral, was engulfed in flames in 2019 in which European city?

15. What is the meaning of the word "wanderlust?"

16. With the help of over **20,000** people and **1,000** elephants, which famous monument was built?

17. With an annual attendance of 58 million people, what is the most visited theme park(s) in the world?

18. What should you do after eating a meal in Egypt to say your compliments to the chef?

19. Who was the first person to ever go skydiving?

20. How long would it take to drive all 50 states in the U.S., assuming there is no traffic?

21. What is the most photographed landmark in the world?

Travel Answers: Landing...

1. **Hong Kong**, China has become the most visited city in the world with over 26.6 million visitors per year!
2. There are over **100,000 flights** per day including passenger, cargo, and military aircraft.
3. **Tokyo, Japan**, is the largest city on Earth, with a population of **37.4 million** people, which is over four times the population of New York City, USA.
4. **The Bahamas'** beach pigs live on Big Major Cay, one of the over 365 islands in Exuma.
5. Crowds battled through the streets of **Spain**, armed with **tomatoes** for the city's annual food fight festival known as **"La Tomatina"**.
6. **Damascus, Syria – 11,000** years old is the oldest city in the world that has seen many of the great civilizations rise and fall.
7. The international land border between the **United States and**

Canada is the longest in the world at almost 8,900 kilometers.

8. The world's largest pyramid lies in **Cholula, Mexico.** The Great Pyramid of Cholula is about 217 feet tall with a base of 1,476 by 1,476 feet.

9. Every year, millions of families run for the nearest KFC in **Japan** and order bucket loads of fried chicken.

10. The busiest airport in the world is **Atlanta**'s Hartsfield-Jackson International Airport. In 2022, **45.4 million** passengers boarded commercial aircraft in Atlanta, Georgia.

11. **Mount Everest**'s peak is the highest altitude above sea level at **29,029 feet**.

12. "The Big Easy" is a popular name for the American city of **New Orleans, Louisiana** because of the relaxed atmosphere there.

13. **College Park Airport** in College Park, Maryland, US, is the world's oldest airport, established in 1909 when Wilbur Wright arrived to train military officers in the Army.

14. A structural fire broke out in the roof space of Notre Dame in **Paris, France**.

15. Wanderlust is a **strong desire** or impulse **to** wander or **travel and explore the world**.

16. **The Taj Mahal** built between 1631 and 1648 is the jewel of Muslim art **in India**.

17. **Disney World** (Magic and Animal Kingdom, Hollywood Studios, EPCOT combined)

18. **Burping** is often considered the highest compliment a guest can pay the host and taking **second helpings** is also considered a sincere compliment. Don't mind if I do!

19. The inventor of the parachute, **André-Jacques Garnerin**, was the first person to successfully jump with a frame less parachute attached to a gondola **in 1797** in Paris.

20. This road trip will take about **224 hours** (9.33 days) of driving in

total, so it's truly an epic undertaking that will take at least **2-3 months** to complete.

21. The most photographed monument in the world is **the Eiffel Tower,** in Paris, France.

Next, we're setting sail to the final chapter where we wrap up our trivia journey with reflections and insights. Join us as we look back on the voyage of knowledge and amusement!

18

Conclusion - The End of Our Trivia Expedition

And so, we reach the final page of our extraordinary trivia odyssey, "Everyday Trivia: Bringing the Brain Back to Life." What a journey it has been! From the corners of everyday life to the majestic mysteries of science and technology, we've traveled through a landscape rich with astonishing facts and delightful surprises. We've explored the realms of sports, marveled at the wonders of nature, indulged in the delicious details of food and drink, and celebrated the magic of movies and entertainment. Our minds have been expanded by the marvels of music, intrigued by the twists and turns of world history, and fascinated by the diverse cultures and traditions that enrich our world.

As we've navigated through the chapters, each one has offered a unique window into the vast and varied tapestry of human knowledge and the world around us. We've laughed, pondered, and perhaps even gasped in amazement at the incredible facts and tales that make our world so endlessly fascinating. From **arts and literature** to the thrill of **travel and adventure**, each page has been a step on a journey of discovery and joy.

But our adventure doesn't have to end here. The beauty of trivia is that it's a never-ending well of knowledge and amusement. There is always more to learn, more to explore, and more to wonder at. I encourage you to continue this journey in your everyday life, to keep the flame of curiosity alive, and to share the fun and wonder with those around you.

As we close this book, I invite you to take a moment to share your thoughts. **Your reviews and feedback on Amazon are immensely appreciated**, as they help others embark on this delightful journey of trivia. Your insights and experiences are valuable and can guide fellow trivia enthusiasts on their path of exploration and fun.

Thank you for joining me on this incredible journey through "Everyday Trivia: Bringing the Brain Back to Life." May your days be filled with wonder, learning, and laughter! Until our next adventure, keep the spirit of curiosity alive!

Thank
You!

www.ingramcontent.com/pod-product-compliance
Lightning Source LLC
Chambersburg PA
CBHW050835260726
48660CB00006B/2259